# What's inside the box?

Author & Illustrator
Angela Stelfox

# What's Inside The Box?

First edition May 2021

Angela Stelfox Be.raptured.giftshop@gmail.com

ISBN: 9781777710521

# Can you guess

## What's inside the box?

# What's inside the box?

They comes in many colours and varieties.

They grow in the ground.
There are tons in the country but you'll even find them in the cities.

Even in special stores they can be found.

Grandmas like to plant them.
They're even nice to smell.
Bees use them to make honey.
Some trees have them as well!

# What's inside the box?

# What's inside the box?

They are always red and juicy.

They have tons of little seeds.

They always grow on bushes.

Their tops are little green leaves.

They love to grow in summer.

They are yummy to eat!

You can put them in a smoothie.

No... it's not a beet!

Did you guess strawberries? 😊 ✅

# What's inside the box?

It has 4 legs and it's furry.
Sometimes they do tricks.
No, it's Not a wolf!
But they love to fetch sticks.
Sometimes they shake a paw.
They love to run and play.
They love bones a treats.
Nope, they don't eat hay!

# Did you guess a dog or a puppy? ✓

# What's inside the box?

They are always round but
vary in size.
Most bounce, some you throw
and others you kick.
They come in many colours.
Some you hit with a stick.
You can take them to the beach.
Toss them over a net.
Or throw them in a basket.
Have you guessed it yet?

# Did you guess a ball?

# What's inside the box?

You wear it on your head.

Some are just for fun.

There are different kinds
for different events.

It can protect you from the sun.

It's great for a hot day.

To prevent a burn on your face.

Cowboys put them on.

Some are fancy with lace.

# Did you guess a hat?

# What's inside the box?

It floats when filled with helium?
Sometimes you get them for your
birthday.
We can fill them with water at the
water park to play.
We throw darts at them to win a prize
at the yearly fair.
On special occasions we give them
because we care.
Some say, "it's a boy" and some say
"get well".
Nope... They don't have a smell!

# What's inside the box?

It is a shape...

Usually they are red.

You have one in your body.

Nope... Not in your head!

It's hiding in your chest.

It's not a diamond or a square.

It makes you think of love.

It's a symbol that you care...

# What's in the box?

It opens and is filled with pages.

Sometimes with words and information.

Sometimes with maps and pictures.

They have them for all different ages.

We read them at school
and before we go to bed.

Some have recipes for cooking.

I'm sure there's many that you have
read...

# Did you guess a book?

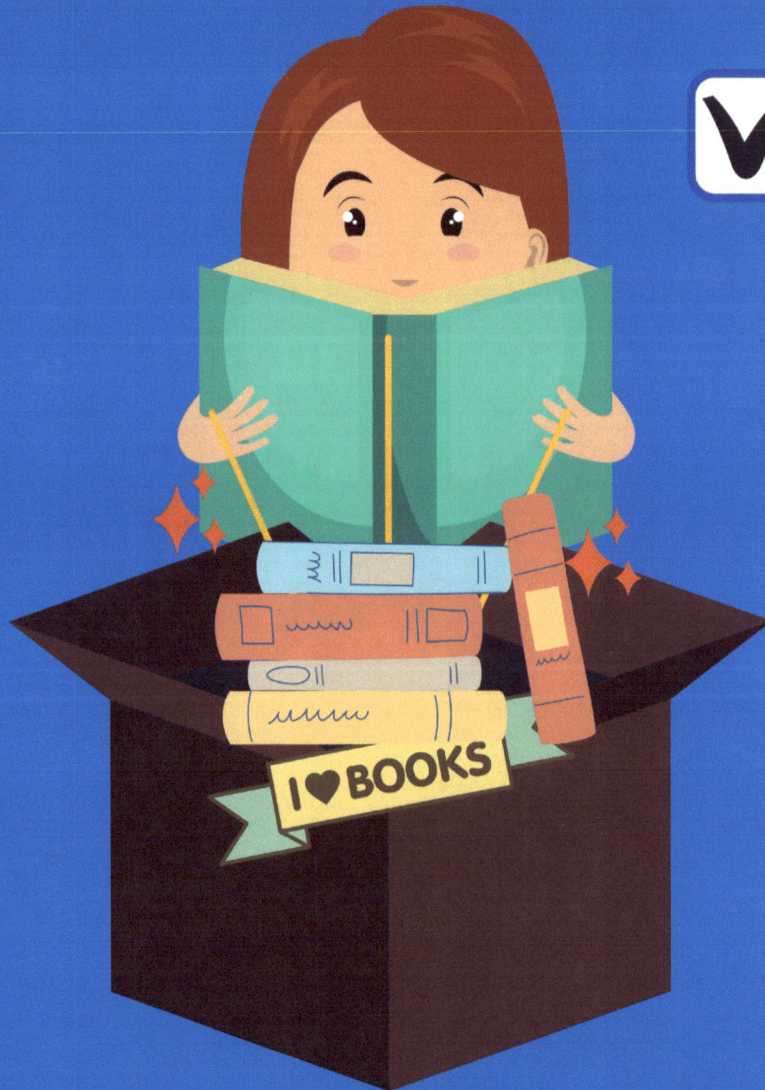

# What's inside the box?

It comes down the tracks, and
says, "Choo Choo"...
People ride on them,
they transport stuff too.
They have a conductor,
and sometimes we have to wait.
When they pass by the street
with many cars of freight.

# Did you guess a train?

# What's inside the box?

They have wings and fly.
Sometimes they are white,
sometimes they are blue.
Their wings match on each side.
They come from a caterpillar
cocoon.
First they crawl with many legs.
Then they hide away.
After a little while
they grow and fly away.

# Did you guess Butterfly? ✓

# What's inside the box?

It is a letter!
The Second one in the
Alphabet...
It comes after A
and before the letter C.
It's fits right in between,
and rhymes with tea...

# Did you guess the letter B? ✓

# What's inside the box?

You can take it to the beach.
You can fill it up with sand.
You can fill it up with water;
hold the handle in your hand.
Sometimes the store has them
full of ice cream.
My mom uses it to mop the floor;
full of soap and bubbles
but that's my least
favourite chore.

# Did you guess a bucket? ✔